HEART SONGS

20 ARRANGEMENTS FOR LADIES' CHOIR OR ENSEMBLE

BY JOSEPH LINN

ENGRAVED BY
DAVID McDONALD

lillenas
PUBLISHING COMPANY

CONTENTS

Hosanna

C. J. R.

CATHY JEFFERS RISSE
Arr. by Joseph Linn

13 might-y, De-fend-er, His ban-ner goes___ be-fore; Sing your

prais-es to___ the King of kings and Lord, the Lord of lords.__

Ho-

CD: 03

I will___ re-joice in the

bless-ing and hon - or, glo-ry and pow - er to Him for-ev - er-more. His

king-dom is e-ter - nal, from age to age____ the same. Let there be

bless-ing and hon - or, glo-ry and pow - er. Wor-ship and a-dore the

ev-er-last - ing name I____ will praise Him! Hal-le - lu-jah!

CD: 05

His Strength Is Perfect

S. C. C. and J. S.

STEVEN CURTIS CHAPMAN
and JERRY SALLEY
Arr. by Tom Fettke
S.S.A. arr. by Joseph Linn

In the First Light

B. K.

BOB KAUFLIN
Arr. by Tom Fettke
S.S.A. arr. by Joseph Linn

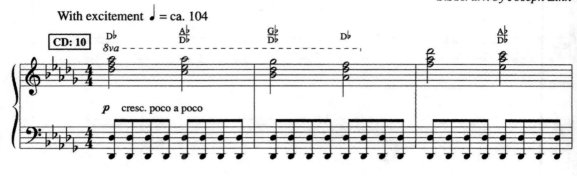

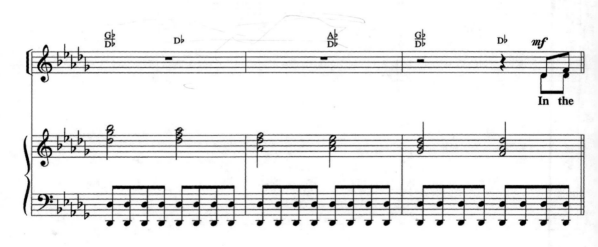

Lyrics:
man. He would tell them of His king-dom, but their

hearts would not be-lieve. They would hate Him and in

an-ger they would nail Him to a tree.

But the sad-ness would be

How Great the Love

D. W.

DAN WHITTEMORE
Arr. by Joseph Linn

Chil-dren of God___ born not of flesh___ but of spir-

CD: 15

-it.

And what shall be___ in time

I know that He will make known.

And some-day I'll

see Him as He is___ And I know___ that I,___ I shall be

plete, it fills and it o - ver - flows–

smoother

Not just in time, but for e - ter - ni -

ty– A - bove and be - yond an-y love that this

detached

world can show. His love is

smoother

8va - - - ┘

Eternal Life

St. FRANCIS of ASSISI (1182-1226)

OLIVE DUNGAN
Arr. by William Stickles
S.S.A. arr. by Joseph Linn

par - don; Where there is doubt, faith;

Where there is de - spair, hope;_____ Where there is dark - ness,

CD: 21   rall.

light; Where there is sad - ness, joy._____

a tempo

O Di - vine Mas - ter, grant that I may not so much

seek_____ To be con-soled_____ as to con - sole,_____ To be

un - der-stood_____ as to un-der - stand,_____ To be loved as to

CD: 22

love;_____ For it is in giv - ing that

rit. *mf* a tempo

we re - ceive;_____ It is in

cresc. poco a poco

par - d'ning   that   we   are   par - doned;   It

is _____ in   dy - ing   that   we   are   born _____

to   e - ter - nal   life. _____

Embrace the Cross

J. E.

JOHN ELLIOTT
Arr. by Joseph Linn

trea - sure; E - ter - ni - ty can't mea - sure what Je - sus holds in

trea - sure; E - ter - ni - ty can't mea - sure what Je - sus holds in

CD: 25

store. Em - brace the love_____ the cross re -

store. Em - brace the love_____ the cross re -

quires;_____ Cling to the One whose heart knew ev - 'ry

quires;_____ Cling to the One whose heart knew ev - 'ry

Je - sus, make us bold - er

To face with cour - age the shame and dis - grace You

CD: 27

bore up - on Your shoul - der. Em - brace the

mor-row   your cross of suf-fer-ing. _____   Em-brace the

mor-row   your cross of suf-fer-ing. _____   Em-brace the

cross.   Em-brace the   cross, _____   the won-drous

cross,   the   cross   of   Je   -   sus.

The Blood Will Never Lose Its Power

A. C.

ANDRAE CROUCH
Arr. by Joseph Linn

1. The blood that my Je - sus shed_____ for me,
(2. It) soothes my doubts_____ and calms_____ my

me,
fears,

'Way back on_____
And it dries_____

CD: 29 — 1st time; CD: 31 — 2nd time

I Surrender All

JUDSON W. VAN DEVENTER

WINFIELD S. WEEDEN
and JOSEPH LINN
Arr. by Joseph Linn

50

We Shall Rise

D. W.

DAN WHITTEMORE
Arr. by Joseph Linn

52

I Bowed on My Knees and Cried, "Holy!"

Anon.

E. M. DUDLEY CANTWELL
Arr. by Joseph Linn

CD: 42

scenes were too num-'rous to tell. I saw A-bra-ham, I-saac, and

scenes num-'rous num-'rous to tell.

Ja-cob,____ Mark, Luke, and Tim-o-thy;____ But I

Ah,__ Mark, Luke Oo____ But I

mel.

CD: 44

said, "I want to see Je-sus,____ The One____ who died____ for

said, "Je-sus, One____ who died____ for

mel. in 2nd sop.

of the Lord. I bowed down and wor-shiped Je - ho- vah,_____ My

Friend of Cal - va - ry._____ I want - ed to give praise to

Je - sus_____ For sav - ing a sin - ner like__ me._____ I

I'm Bound for the Kingdom

M. L.

MOSIE LISTER
Arr. by Joseph Linn

With feeling ♩. = ca. 96
mel. in 2nd sop.
mf

1. You may ask me____ where I'm head - ed;____ you may
ask me____ where I'm head - ed;____ you may

ask me____ where I'm bound.____ Well, I'm go - ing____ to a
ask me____ where I'm bound.____ go - ing____ to a

coun - try____ 'cross the sea, 'cross the sea.____ And I
coun - try____ 'cross the sea, 'cross the sea.____

know I'll____ have a man - sion,____ and_ I know I'll____ have a
know I'll____ have a man - sion,____ and I know I'll____ have a

Bless God

J. R. and C. L.

JOHN ROSASCO and
CARMAN LICCIARDELLO
Arr. by Joseph Linn

2 CD: 50

sing, "Bless___ God!" Bless God___ for

all He's done! Bless God___ for Christ, His Son!

Let us mag - ni - fy Him for He's ho - ly,

ho - ly! One voice___ in u - ni - ty, one

Ah Lord God

Hallelujah, Amen
Ah Lord God

Arr. by Joseph Linn

CD: 51 With a sense of awe ♩ = ca. 86
tacet through measure 50

* "Hallelujah, Amen" (Whittemore)

Lord, who can list Thy

Lord, who can list Thy

glo-rious deeds? Lord, who gives right-ful praise?

glo-rious deeds? Lord, who gives right-ful praise?

O for a Thousand Tongues

D. B.

DAVID BINION
Arr. by Bill Wolaver
S.S.A. arr. by Joseph Linn

1. Glo - ry to the Lamb,_____ whose throne for - ev - er reigns;_____

God in the high - est, _____

CD: 56

wor - thy to mer - it our ___ praise. _____

O for a thou - sand tongues to sing

mel. in 2nd sop.

prais - es un - to Thee; _____

praise _____ In hum-ble ad - o -

ra - tion, _____ in end - less _____ re -

frain, end - less re - frain. _____

O for a thou - sand tongues to sing prais - es

He Will Pilot Me

CHARLES T. BAILEY

BYRON L. WHITWORTH
Arr. by Joseph Linn

* Option: use same soloist throughout

One Small Child

D. M.

DAVID MEECE
Arr. by Joseph Linn

See the kings on bend - ed knee, See the moth - er
prais - ing the Fa - ther, See the bless - ed In - fant sleep.

CD: 70

One small child in a land of a thou - sand, One small dream in a

We Praise Thee, O God Our Redeemer

JULIA C. CORY

Netherlands Folksong
Arr. by Doug Holck
S.S.A. arr. by Joseph Linn

18 bless Thy ho - ly name; _____ glad prais - es we sing.

L. H. detached

22 CD: 72

mp

decresc.

2. We

26 wor - ship Thee; God of our fa - thers, we bless Thee. Through

mp

30 mf

life's storm and tem - pest our guide Thou hast been. _____ When

cresc.

mf

per - ils o'er - take us Thou wilt____ not for - sake us; And

with Thy help, O Lord,____ life's____ bat - tles we__ win.

3. With

Thee, to Thee, our great Re - deem - er, for - ev - er be____ praise.

Thee, our great Re - deem - er, for - ev - er____ be praise.

A - men, a - men, a -

A - men, a - men,

- men, a - men,____ a - men, a - men, a - men.

a - men, a - men,____ a - men, a - men, a - men.

There Is a Fountain

with "Nothing But the Blood"

Arr. by Joseph Linn

is a foun - tain filled with blood drawn_ from Im-man - uel's_

veins,_____ And_ sin - ners plunged be - neath that flood lose_

all their guilt - y_ stains. The_ dy - ing thief re -

joiced to see that_ foun - tain in_ his_ day,_____ And

all my sins a - way,_____ wash___ all my sins a -

way,_____ And___ there may I, tho'___ vile as he, wash___

all my sins a - way._____ And___ there may I, tho'___

Wash___ all my sins a - way, wash a -

vile as he, wash___ all my sins, What can wash a -

When We Hear the Trumpet Sound

M. L.

MOSIE LISTER
Arr. by Mosie Lister
S.S.A. arr. by Joseph Linn

Rest Within His Sanctuary

D. W.

DAN WHITTEMORE
Arr. by Joseph Linn

do I thank___ God___ for re-lease?_____ Why? Be-cause I___

know He___ loves me, and by faith I en-ter in___

To the safe-ty___ of His___re-fuge, where He saves me from my___

sin.___ He brings com-fort to the suf-f'ring,

CD: 84

strength to those_____ lost and a-lone; For He of-fers_____

an a-sy-lum, call-ing us___ to___ be His own.

Lis-ten, you can___ hear Him___ call-ing from the cross and

emp-ty grave,_____ "En-ter in My___ sanc-tu-ar-y;